I Survived the HOLOCAUST

MY LIFE IN POETRY

Renate Kaufmann

I Survived the HOLOCAUST
MY LIFE IN POETRY

ISBN **978-0-9855241-2-8**

1. Poetry: inspirational and religious

2. Autobiography : Historical - Holocaust

3. Religion: Messianic Judaism

Cover pencil drawing, copyright © 2012 the author, drawn by her father when he was in a Holocaust containment camp.
All interior artwork copyright © 2012 by the author, except for:
Image p. 31 copyright © 2012 by shutterstock.com, used by permission.
Photos pp. 8,9,32,33 copyright © 2012 by Cheryl Zehr
Father-son drawing p. 33 copyright © 2012 by Karen Van Lieu
9-11 photo p. 62 courtesy wikipedia, public domain

Cover and interior design, copyright © 2012 by Chery Zehr, Olive Press

Published by
Olive Press
Messianic and Christian Publisher
www.olivepresspublisher.com
olivepressbooks@gmail.com

OlivePress
צהר | זית
Messianic & Christian Publisher

The art images are grayscale photos of beautiful pieces of artwork of various media done by the author. All are in vibrant colors except for the the pencil drawings and her border art of which the originals are black and white.

Our prayer at Olive Press is that we may help make the Word of Adonai fully known, that it spread rapidly and be glorified everywhere. We hope our books help open people's eyes so they will turn from darkness to Light and from the power of the adversary to God and to trust in ישוע Yeshua (Jesus). (From II Thess. 3:1; Col. 1:25; Acts 26:18,15 NRSV *New Revised Standard Version* and CJB *Complete Jewish Bible*) May this book in particular help to bring unity and understanding among believers.

Dedication

Throughout my life, there have been so many wonderful things that could only have come from ELOHIM, therefore I give all the glory to Him.

Poem Contents

What Is Peace?

Mama, what is peace? I asked
When we suffered World War II;
Mama, why do we have to wear a star?
My child, because you are a Jew.

Mama, will there again be a time
When angry men will smile?
I hope, my child, it will be soon;
Be strong, hold on and trust awhile.

Trust in what and what is trust?
Trust in hope, my child, that is a must;
Hope in your Maker up above,
The only hope, abundant love.

The only way that there is peace,
When bombs and cruel men will cease
And groceries will fill the shelves,
When one can work and again believe in self.

When people without fear can go to the house of God;
When cities will be rebuilt on every street and corner lot;
When people learn again to smile and call each other sister, brother;
When friends don't betray one's trust but reason with each other.

When hope is stirred to find a way
And love is found in every heart,
When parents raise children to obey
And races are not kept apart.

And encouragement to help will be expressed,
When all mankind can claim and seek togetherness;
When all of us pray and praise our God upon our knees,
Then, my child, and only then, will we experience peace.

I Survived the Holocaust

The war was roaring; the lights turned dim
   A town was shrouded black,
Full fear, but hope...not to be hurt
   By a nightly bomb attack.

My parents warned that in days ahead
   My future would be marked or changed,
By death or by cruel destiny
   By a leader who was deranged.

The warning words I fearfully heard
   Of losing father, or dear mother,
Or even, I could die!
   Still hearing it, I shudder.

My faithful dad taught all he could
   To fill my curious mind:
Behave, my child, avoid the wrong,
   To others, please be kind.

And guard your mouth; for truth still stand
   Walk tall, and do not moan,
So many birds do fly in flocks
    But eagles soar alone.

He taught me that our God is real,
   And even sent His Son,
That in this God-forsaken place
   Still souls through Him are won.

I see Dad in our living room,
   When Mother did explain,
"My child, who knows what comes our way
   When nightly bombs do rain?'

"We might even lose you,
   And sadly must go on,
So many people die before
   A war is lost or won."

Remembering as it were yesterday...
   "Oh no! I will not die
Until I see Yeshua
   Returning in the sky."

"Oh, yes, my child! I hope we all
   Will see Him at last that way."
I still remember it as if
   It were just yesterday.

The war was lost; all hope was tossed,
   My father was no more;
Another Jewish life snuffed out
   Behind a furnace door.

My mother's life was spared
   And long her eyes had tears,
My body had been cruelly marred
   "O God, heal our souls from fears."

She joined me, broken and so ill.
   The war had left its mark,
Yet her bravery exhibited
   A glimmer in the dark.

With wise resolve she warned the men,
   "Give up; wave a bright clean sheet
To save our village from its doom."
   U.S. tanks came up the street.

Mama's leading saved our place
   Of fourteen houses strong,
A guesthouse...waterworks...a mill
   A place just one mile long.

I have so many memories
   This poem might find no end,
Well, I survived and Hitler died
   My life is in God's hands!

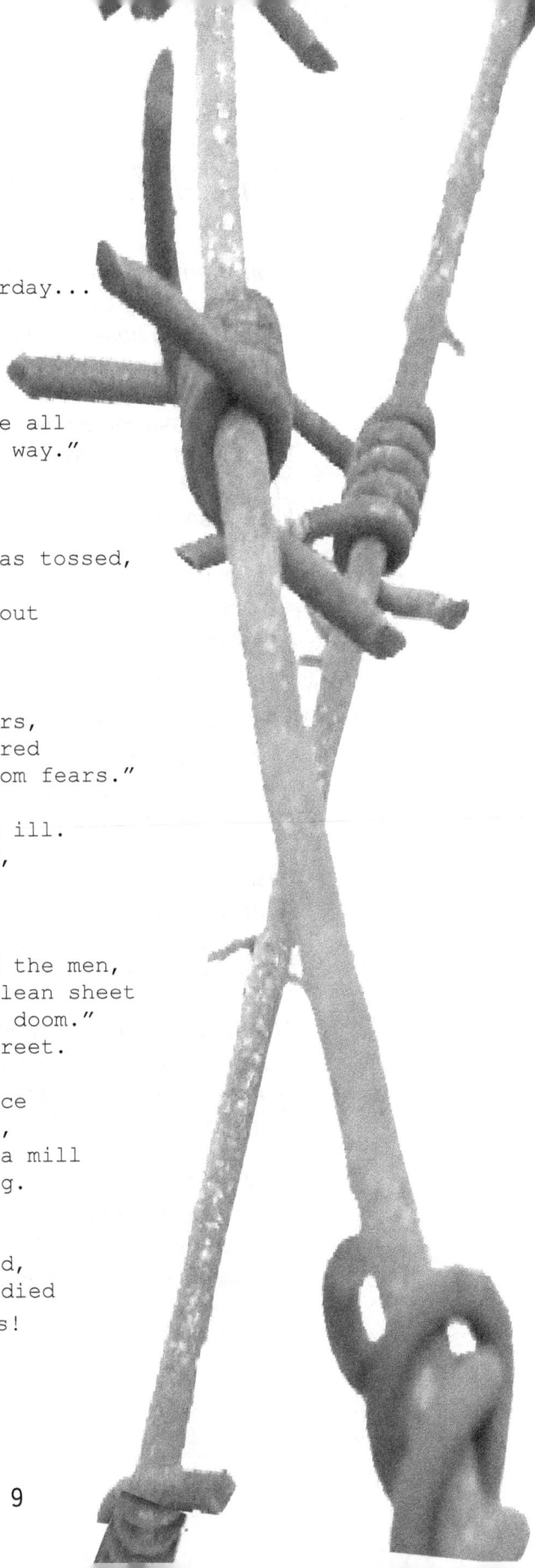

Why Hate the Jews?

From Haman...Stalin...Hitler...
To the final Anti-Christ
There will be haters of us Jews
And God fearers who are wise.

There always will be people who
Want to rid the world of Jews,
The ignorance of haters who
Lack wisdom from the Truth.

But we will walk this earth
'Til our God once more
Revives us from the ashes to
Bless this world from shore to shore.

The word "Jew'" has a precious meaning
Most people know it not,
It means to be a praiser
Of our Father, of our God.

I ask you now, are you
A praiser of Elohim?
Then, you, too are a chosen one!
You know where you fit in.

The answer to this riddle is
 Found in His book of Ruth,
When you fall in love with God
You should also love the Jew.

We are all sisters and brothers
All members of the human race,
Created by our Father God,
And saved only by His grace!

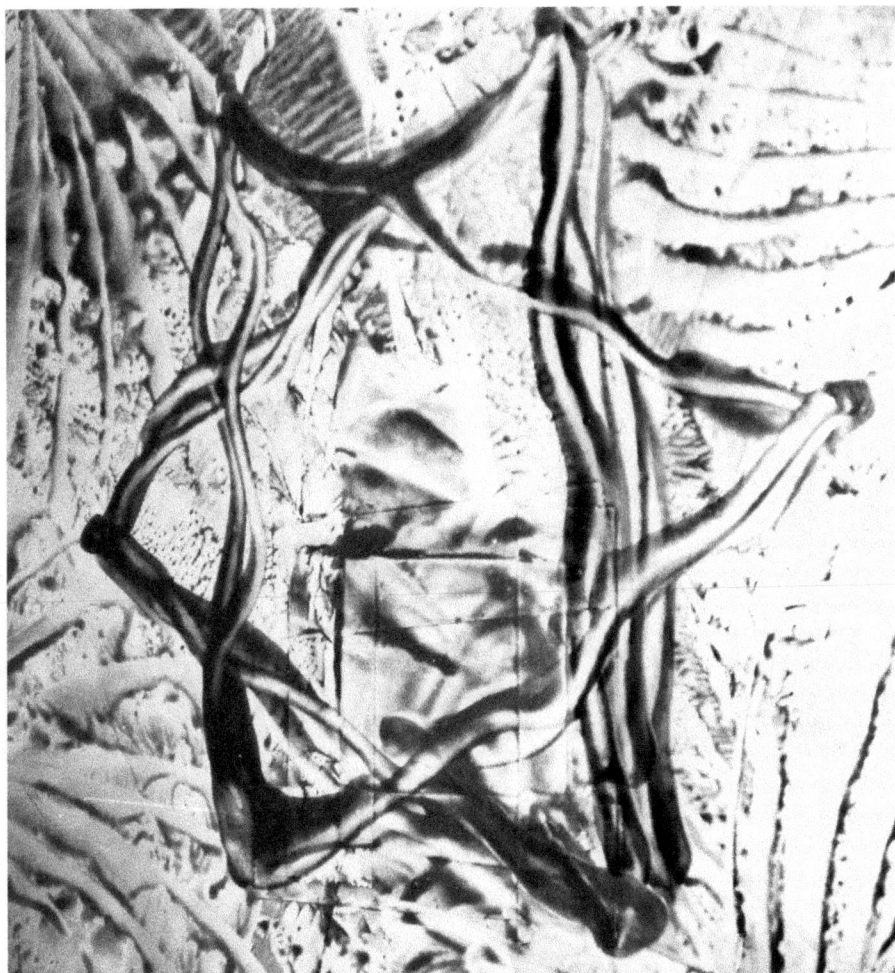

My Hiding Place (1943-45)

My camp was a house in a village quite quaint
A place to hide, but not by a saint,
A place where many fled from the terrors grown
But under this roof was a war of its own.

Prostitution, abortions, physical abuse
Here lived a lady with a very short fuse,
She beat her children, now I was here, too
She beat me unmercifully for things I didn't do.

My back was injured, my mind deranged
So many things this bitter war changed,
My parents away, didn't know if still alive
But mother came for me, father did not survive.

They beat him with rifle butts and split his skull
He died a martyr's death, so vicious and cruel,
We did live on but in spirit and soul
Both broken and marred from life's unrighteous school.

Beloved Switzerland

Oh, my beloved Switzerland
Where the air is so pristine,
Your country showed me wondrous sights
I never before had seen.

Your flowered meadows, so many streams
And highest mountain peaks,
O beautiful land which God once formed
My soul so often seeks.

Here, after years of war
My frame a skeleton with skin,
Hungry in so many ways
Your kindness took me in.

You nourished me by people
Who still had a giving heart,
You showed me that life could be good
A new strength in me did start.

Your houses stood since ancient time
Your people a busy throng,
Full peace and very healthy lives
So opposite where I am from.

Six years of war, a leader mad,
A people dressed in black,
The streets full of rubble and debris,
I wish not to go back.

What Is A Home?

A place where Father hangs his hat,
A romper room where shoes fly when they are wet,
A kitchen to spread fragrance through the house,
Maybe there is a cat to chase a rat or mouse.

The dining room where guests rejoice to celebrate,
Or friends spend time just to debate,
A living room from daily chores to rest
To read a book or knit or even playing chess.

A bathroom, a luxury so good
A bath there by candlelight as often as we could,
The bedroom to rest up from the day,
To be tucked in, after kneeling there to pray.

The basement to put the things we seldom use
On walls, pictures from long ago to amuse.
The attic oft' cluttered with old treasure.
Good for hours of make-believe pleasure.

The landscape outside portrays beautifies the seasons,
You meet your neighbors for all kinds of reasons.
So many occasions a home is for—
A refuge for friends who enter your door.

It is a gift from God to you.
His provisions all came through.
Enjoy your home with blessings filled,
And use it for good—your Father has willed.

(It was in Switzerland that I
experienced this kind of home
which before I had only
dreamed could exist.)

17

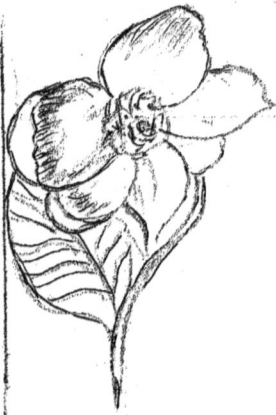

Mama,
Is there Life After Death?

"Mama, is there life after death?"
"Oh yes, my child; there is!
Where do you think that Heaven is?
Up in the blue." And she gave me
            her good-night kiss.

"But Mama, tell me …
What happens when we're gone?"
"Don't worry:
In our children we will live on."

Yes, that was fifty years ago.
Mama's gone some years,
            And I still miss her so.

But not only our parents live on
            In our memory file:
There are pastors; rabbis; teachers
Who crowned our lives a precious while.
There were aunts and uncles; neighbors;
Our friends and enemies;
All have formed a rug of life
From each we learned in some degree.

See? We see our callouses
And so many cuts
And twisted knots.
When will we see the finished work
Which formed the heights
            And lowest ruts?

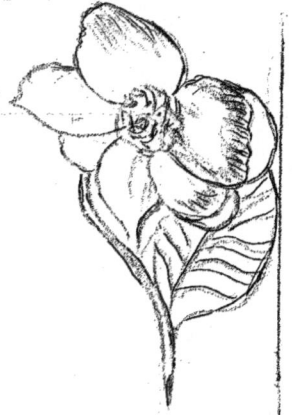

Yes, there are people I recall
Who played a vital part;
Who formed my life by teaching me
Some things so easy, but much was hard.

And then one day when that shofar sounds,
And Yeshua Jesus will appear—
And we stand on that holy mound;
We'll embrace the ones we called so dear.

And there is Mother and my dad.
And hopeful, uncles and my aunts I'll see …
And cousins, friends …
　　　　　　　And no one I'll call my enemy.

And sweet rewards are given us.
A crown is placed on
Our tapestry of strife;
And beautiful designs we see
Which were woven by our ups and downs of life.

Heaven

Looking up in the sky at night

Astonished by the wondrous sight

And think that's the backside of heaven you see,

How much more precious the right side of heaven must be.

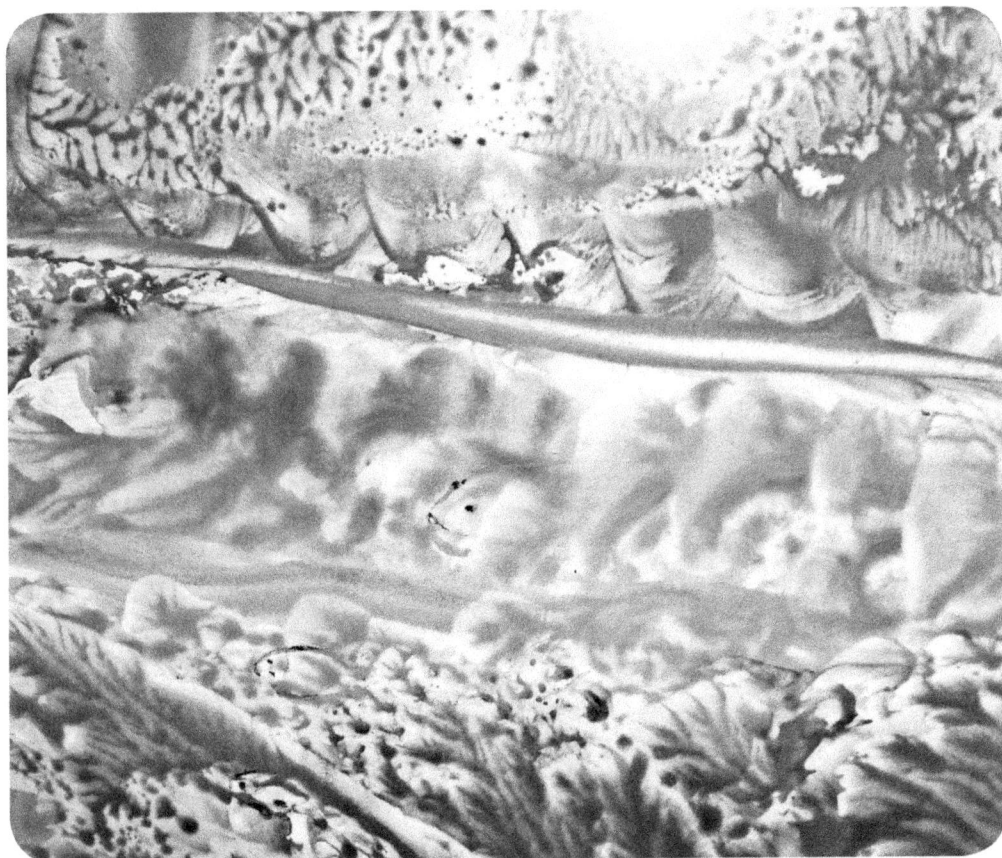

The author's painting of the most beautiful,
brilliant, heavenly shades of blue!

Nani

Could I just steal myself away
And walk with you along the River Rhine,
Relive that melancholic past
Reverse what was and call you mine?

How many times I think of you
Your arms are holding me at last,
Hearing your broken German words
Our future dreams become a lonely past.

Do you sometimes look up at night
To see the starry sky
And think of me across the sea
And regrettingly ask why?

I feel your love though far away
Separated by the years.
Never can I call you mine
Painfully yearning, shedding tears.

My mother said, God bless her soul,
I hear her words so clear,
"When you have found him, hold him tight
And never play with love, my dear."

I held you with all my might, my dove
But family tensions ripped our bond in two
Be well, my handsome Arab love,
You were not allowed to wed a Jew.

Who Am I?

Born in a time when peace was only a word
Where nightly air raids and bombs were heard,
Where people were sober and smiles seldom seen
In this world of chaos I had to fit in.

I grew up in fear, running and hiding
Scared, unimportant, tempers colliding;
Shaking in fear of the daily whip
By my captor's fury, etching scars on my hip.

I suffered long from the years, lived in pain
I longed so for my dad, never saw him again,
I grew up with only four years of school
But I learned what I could, was nobody's fool.

Dressing women in lace and fancy arrays
Designed clothing as seen at my mother's place,
A private college gave me the chance
To further my learning, my knowledge enhanced.

Accounting, a new field, a living to earn
For a special soul-mate my heart now did yearn,
I fell in love with the man of my dreams
But we were ripped apart by political schemes.

He a handsome Arab, I a pretty Jew
Two worlds collided, what was I to do?

Once snatched away from a madman's fury
Now hounded again by two races' jury,
I left my homeland for the U.S. to stay
We still love each other in silence today.

Our lives went on after shattered dreams
I married three times, left husbands with screams;
To a girl I gave birth, a new meaning for life
Now two mouths to feed, new challenge and strife.

Today, after many turbulent years
With laughter and worries and so many tears,
I still manage life with a smile on my face
And depend on God's guidance and His infinite grace.

Now I write down my life in poetry
Paint flowers and things the way I see,
I sing from the bema* to praise God on high
My body aches and deep is my sigh.

Who am I, you ask? I'm a product of survival
Only in God's home I see my final arrival,
I laugh at myself to lessen my pain
Holding on to God is keeping me sane.

*podium or platform

Many Years Later

Many years later I am often asked
Were you scared by the bombs daily blast?
You wore a star to show you're a Jew
What kind of things did they make you do?

Which camps were you in where so few survived
Or other places of normal life deprived?
Did you starve and endure hunger pains?
How much did you lose and later regain?

Well, I was a small child, so scared of war attacks
The few walls remaining were full of cracks,
The city folks fled like scattered lambs
Only the clothes on their backs, gold and diamonds sewed in hems.

In the railway stations, people lay waiting for a train
I slept on a table; others sat in the rain,
Ripped from my sleep, stuffed into a coppel
We went further south, a journey through hell.

Deep in the night changing several trains
Two days more travel, maimed body and brain;
We arrived at a village, now walk further three miles
In a little house we found food, lodging and smiles.

I was left there alone with a family quite strange
My new hiding place by my mother pre-arranged,
Food I could not stomach, my heart full of fear
In unfriendly hands I now had to persevere.

One year-and-a-half my mother returned
She came back from the ashes the cities burned,
My father was murdered by Nazi hands
But my mother's face eased my longing pains.

The bombs had stilled but the hunger grew on
The farmer killed, even the cattle were gone;
The war left a gaping wound all over the land
The women rebuilt and gave each other a hand.

A senseless war, nobody did win.
The ones who survived it lost most of their kin,
Devastation, in ruins was the country's pride
Because of a madman who was not so gescheit.*

Did we learn from that tyrant how to better our lot?
So many did ask, "Where is our God?"
Led in fear, they followed Hitler's call—
A heartless man who almost murdered all.

I hated man now, only my father was good
Why did they kill him, I never understood;
I know he was well when I said my last goodbye.
Now the years that followed, for his love did I cry.

*clever, intelligent, smart

27

What Is Wrong With This World?

Why can't we all live in peace?
Aren't we all sick of this hating disease?
Have we all gone astray from the truth?
Why all the turmoil and hatred of Jews?

I am dissonant, angry and sad.
Why destroy so much of what the Lord has made?
So many lives destroyed by afflicted pain
Oh hope, come quickly so we can live again.

Some never come to see the light
No chance was given for wrong or right,
Ripped by cruel hands out of her belly
And discarded life, trashed into death valley.

Oh God, my God, I call to You
How much more do we have to go through?
How many more years 'til You finally appear?
Which day or month or even which year?

Uncertainty

O Yeshua, do remember me.

When I first walked the lonesome way with Thee,

The days were bright; the worries seemed to fade away

Even though it rained, my heart was full of sunshine every day.

Please, dear Lord, come back to me.

Lift the jungle of uncertainty.

I Found The Truth

Already hard were the times when I was born, and cruel;
The war began when I was 2, and at 6 I went to school.
But short lived was my eager start--
I was denied the privilege of learning and getting smart.
And nothing there was that we could do,
"We educate the Aryan race, and not a dirty Jew."

So mother crossed the land with me to find a hiding place;
A tiny spot was needed, a humble little space.
The war was roaring, so many times our life was spared;
The country air was fresh, and meager food with me was shared.
My father's life unjustly taken,
And mothers' mind and body shaken.

When the war was over, and Hitler finally dead,
We crawled out from the ashes, and straw was our bed.
Four blocks to get our water, we made do with what we found;
So glad were we to survive, 8 people in 2 rooms, family united bound.
The struggle was not over; the city was destroyed,
But bravery and eagerness replaced the gloomy void.

The women started rebuilding; the men returned from fighting;
Yet very frail and frightened after years in camps and hiding.
Our minds were crippled, our souls burned out.
Will happiness ever return? Is there a healer above the cloud?
I never stopped my praying, and often prayed so hard,
"Please heal my broken body and mind; please give me a new start."

God heard my cry, and Switzerland became my healing place
When I was 10, I started school again, in many different ways.
With sins, dismay, pain and many tears
Did I survive my teenage years.
There was no love, I stood alone—
Worthless, depressed, my will for life was gone.

I remembered my father's love, so honest and so good.
Why could he not stay guiding me? I never understood.
Oh my God, my heart is drained, so many men have come and gone.
Is there not one for me You choose with whom I can go on?
So many did I know, so shallow were their lives
Not one of them I wanted, I knew too many unhappy wives.

I have to find the Truth, if there is such a thing.
I searched and asked, "Is there a source that truth to me can bring?"
But what is truth? All I knew were lies.
I know there is an evil one, with a cunning and sly disguise.
"But God," I prayed, "Where can I find the Truth there is for life?
I must find her, I must know her, down here, just to survive."

I left my home, my family and my lover from the past.
In Denver or in Alaska? No, in Rochester I found the Truth at last.
At Petah Tikvah did I learn the way of Jewish kin;
The Holy Days, how to be kept, a walk in truth avoiding sin.
Hear, O Israel, a place where ears will hear,
Where God is worshipped in Messianic song with enthusiastic cheer.

Come, let us celebrate our new-found life in Him
Who loved us, gave His life for us, to free us from our sin.
He promised us eternal life through His redemptive story,
Dimensions not yet known to us, all Truth and honesty and glory.

A Peculiar People

A peculiar people in this world
Their gain so high in cost,
With payment that was dearly spent
When all their lives they lost.

Some still adhere to the precious call
Brought from the One of Old,
He gave His word so we would know
To make us strong and bold.

We do things backward from the world
We write from right to left,
And from the back we open books
Even one struck water from a cleft.

We celebrate so many feasts
The Lord proclaimed a few,
We do so many things strangely
That's why we're called a Jew.

We count our time since Abraham
Who started this peculiar folk,
When God had promised blessings to flow
We chose to carry a heavy yoke.

But our Father remembers us
And His great love we know,
He calls us back into our land
Where milk and honey flow.

We blessed the world by roaming it
Wrote books that life and justice taught;
We shed light on life in humorous way
And freed the lands in wars we fought.

Well, I have found the answer here
It was written clearly in His book,
Even though He wanted His best for us
His good guidance we forsook.

Today, we long to return to Him
This, too, it was foretold,
To bring us back into the land
From ancient times so old.

So many of our hearts are maimed
And some are hard like stone,
But this is not a Jewish plight
Here, we do not stand alone.

He called us back into our Land
Where Yahwah's feasts are kept,
Here learning of the Godly things
With blessings we accept.

He called us back to ancient grounds
Where Yeshua's feet once stood,
And now we are His Sabbath Bride
Redeemed by God's Son's blood.

Who is on the Lord's Side?

You call yourself a Christian? Do you know where you stand?
Do you follow wrong standards? Or do you give Israel a hand?
We must remember what God once said:
He who does not love Israel will be cursed instead.
A warning Christians: learn what to do,
The good Book you believe in was delivered by the Jew.
Only ignorance denies the way you must choose,
You can't be a blessing if you hate the Jews.
It is said that one day—maybe in a short while
All the Jews will return on the wings of the Gentiles.
Please look into your Bible and learn of things to come,
When you call yourself a Christian, you too must be a chosen one.
The inheritance you claim was not yours at first,
The plan of salvation is truly of Jewish birth.
We must unite our efforts, knit together as a chain
So God can pour out His promised latter rain.
The concoction is brewed for more wars to come,
The world paves the road to Armageddon.
We are calling for peace, but war we sow.
Wake up Christian world! Watch the way you should go.
Don't take your support of Israel for granted.
Are you for God or are you petroleum slanted?
Please study the Book delivered by the Jew!
It will answer the question: On which side is God putting you?

On the left go the goats, on the right His enduring sheep,
His love reaches to heaven but His fury is deep.
Now, I ask you again: Who is on God's righteous side?
Will you be with Zion and be His beloved bride?

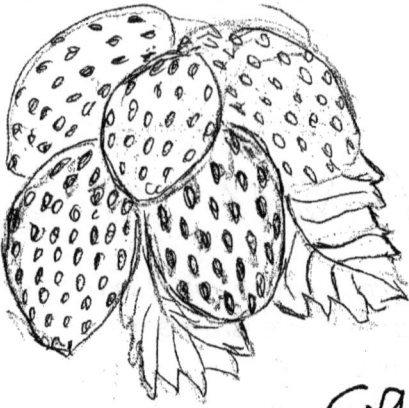

I Love My Garden the Best

Thank You, Lord, for my lovely home
A haven of rest, a shelter from storm,
A place for friends to share my day
And a place for wayward ones to stay.

A place I call mine in the midst of town
Where boom box noise often makes me frown,
The children grow up not always so nice
The modern world has to pay its price.

Now sixteen years have come and gone
I know some neighbors, but not everyone,
Here people live in a private way
We build high fences, divided we stay.

We greet and talk, briefly converse
I know we should love each other here on earth,
But private we live, listen and see
All have separate ways: "Don't bother me."

But all in all I'm happy here
My postage stamp lot brings me so much cheer,
I planted a garden to many a delight
Where colorful flowers are shining bright.

A pond with fishes quicken one's mood
And bowls and dishes with animal food,
A pavilion in back where I prayerfully rest
I really love my garden the best.

Some neighbors stop when by they walk
Peeking through the driveway, sometimes we talk,
I invite them in to share my fauna blessed
Smiling, they say, "I like your garden best."

So God has blessed since I came to New York
I started a new life, and hard I worked;
He gave me a home I love to share
His blessings follow me everywhere.

Not an Alien Anymore

I am not an alien anymore
Yes, once I came from a far away shore,
I bought a ticket that I saved for
And by ship I came to America's door.

Now here I saw a future grand
I came to you to serve this land,
I really fell in love with you
You taught me much, but I suffered too.

I earned American citizenship
With new language learned, some words I skip,
My accent, well, I tried to lose
But, you try to walk in German shoes.

I am proud to be an American
With apple pie and handsome men,
And girls, my friends, I dearly love
Who taught me to know the One above.

I owe you thanks to be my friends
To trust in me with no demands,
To love me just for who I am
I now belong—I'm an American.

Thank God

Thank God You gave me friends who came
To love me just for me; just friendships reign.
They pray for me for health and peace to share
A warm embrace, I do feel loved again.

Thank God for all You let me have
A home so quaint, so beautiful;
My animals, too, add to my life
And people share it; my days never dull.

Thank God I spend the quiet times with You,
Your mercy gives me life, not hell;
You took the cross for me—You suffered through,
You are my life, I know it well.

So keep on walking with me, my God
I humbly ask, I need Your hand,
I read Your Word, yet know it not
Please keep me close when the day is spent.

A Transparent Servant

My God, give me clarity of mind
Remembering my faltering past,
I want to undo where oft' I was unkind.
Implant in me a servant's heart at last.

Let me be willing to endure
The flood of life's endless demands,
But comfort me so I can be sure
That through it all with You I firmly stand.

Give strength to fight the test of time
And calm my turmoiled soul,
I want to be Yours, let me know I'm Thine
To please You is my only goal.

Undo the deepened groove by sin
Rebuild me with Your virtuous life,
That victory I will have within
And now graciously manage strife.

Alter my ways, shine Your light through me
No more deceit or cunning manipulation,
And wash my soul transparently
Make me pure as You at Your transfiguration.

I Am A Messianic Jew

I am a Messianic Jew
Not a Christian or Catholic or Protestant
But yet we all reach out to His loving hand

Li li li li li ...

We believe the Messiah will come again
And from Jerusalem, He will finally reign
We are waiting with anticipation,
all over the nations

Li li li li li ...

We believe He came to take our sin
To bring us back become his kin
He shed His blood to set us free
and forever more with Him to be

Li li li li li ...

Wake up you Jews and all human race
He is the One. Now seek His face.
He is the ben Joseph and ben David.
He is my father. I am His kid.

Li li li li li ...

Read in Isaiah 53 and Psalm 22
You find He was the promised Jew
To bring salvation and forgiveness of sin.
He is our brother. We are His kin.

Li li li li li ...

Rejoice with me that He's alive.
He came down to see our suffering and strife
He asked us to trust Him. He sounds the alarm.
He reaches down His loving arm.

Li li li li li …

Here is the patience of the saints
Here are they who took their stand
Even been killed; they feared not to die
They trust His words; they do know why.

Li li li li li …

For a thousand years still on this earth
He shows us how to live in peace
He rights the wrong;
takes away all bad memories

Li li li li li …

And in the end for just once more
He lets the devil loose
To show the Universe that He is just
and the devil pays his dues.

Li li li li li …

Then He will take us to lofty heights
To places we have never been
To meet our Father, we take the flight
like Eagles to be with Him.

Ode To The Proselyte

To be a Yehuda, a praiser of God,
For this you don't need real Jewish blood...
For this you need a Jewish heart.
To love Yeshua is the start,
Becoming the one to join His fold
Fulfills His calling, He who is of old.

You then will belong to the chosen race.
But chosen for what? Pardon this phrase...
Chosen for what the generations have undone.
To worship and praise the Holy One,
To tell the world of His merciful Son.
Of the redemption He brought, our victory He won.
To be chosen to be a Jew means proclaiming His Name
To unite all mankind to make Him their aim.

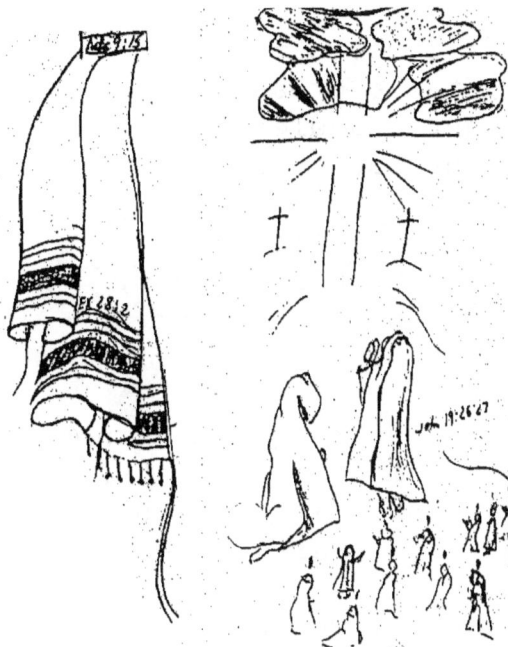

Sabbath Song

Sabbath rest, Sabbath bride
God with us in special might,
Holy rest, children blessed
Celebrate Shabbat tonight.

Holy day of Sabbath rest
Sanctified, table dressed
God our light, candles bright
Celebrate Shabbat tonight.

Let our hearts be lifted up
Eat the Challah, fill the cup,
Rest is here, healing cheer
Sabbath, holy night so dear.

These special hours guard earnestly
Day hallowed for all eternity,
Gift of Sabbath, day of gladness
Day of joy from every sadness.

Lord of Sabbath, we welcome You
With friends and family, too,
Come celebrate with us at home
Let us enjoy Shabbat Shalom.

Shalom to You

It's Sabbath night, the week is done
    The candles softly glow,
The week was hard, but now I rest
    I know God loves me so.

He gave us rest the seventh day
    He blessed and hallowed it,
So we enjoy with family
    The holy Sabbath gift.

"Shabbat Shalom," I say to you,
    A day of calmness to refresh
We dance and sing and worship, too
    We like this day the best.

He gave Himself so we might rest
    For all eternity,
Here now He is, that we might be
    In Sabbath harmony.

Passover

The Hebrews moaned, Yeshua heard their cry
For forty years did Moses sigh;
He saw a burning bush that was not consumed
God saved the Hebrews; the Egyptians were doomed.

This was the beginning of the Passover tradition
A feast to remember God's holy commission,
To teach our children what God had blessed
A day to remember we were saved from distress.

Three thousand years ago our freedom was birthed
And a thousand years later Yeshua walked this earth,
So let us remember and continue on
To show our children what God has done.

He knows the day when He'll return
And for His entrance our hearts do yearn,
So let us remember the Passover Lamb
Who calls Himself the great "I Am".

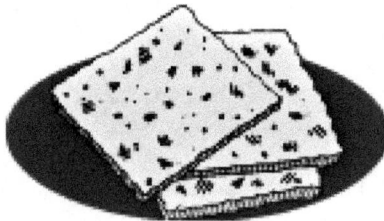

וטו תדותנו

Happy Passover
by RK 93

Without the passing through the Red Sea
There might not be you
But there would not be me.
The plagues shoved of the night from on high
With death and darkness, snake frog and fly
Believe me it was no hokus pokus
God sends the water the wind and the locusts
He is able to do unimagenable things
He can shelter or carry you on His wings
Jesuah the cloud by day and fire at night
With a Temple of cloth seen from every sight

Passover is one of His glorious days
where we remember His doings
in such wonderous ways.
How He called us together
from bondage He wrought
So we know He is Jehovah
the only true God

with love Renate

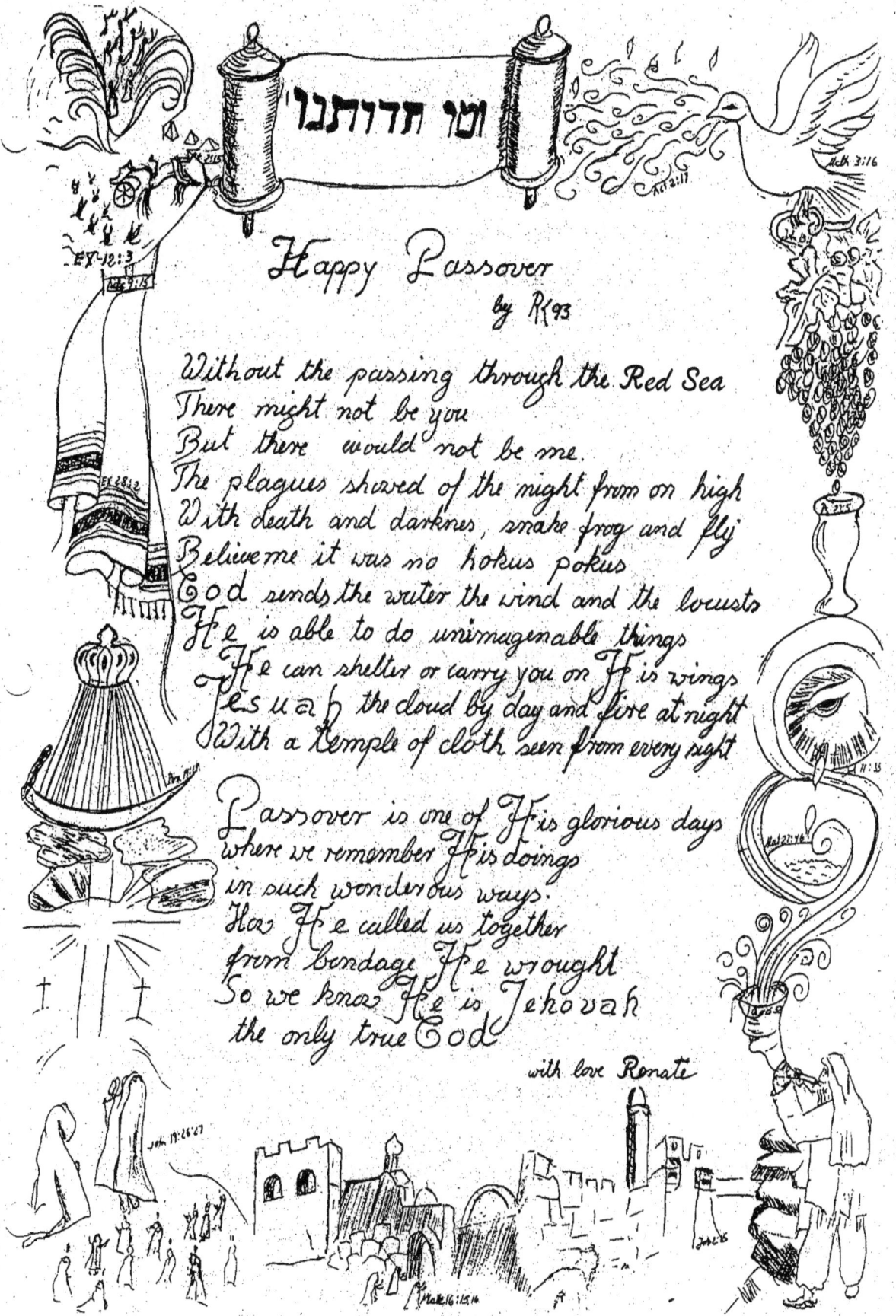

Exodus

Moses declined to be the next in line
As Egypt's Pharaoh, earthly power and fame
Instead, for 40 years he herded sheep
Until the day he saw a bush aflame.

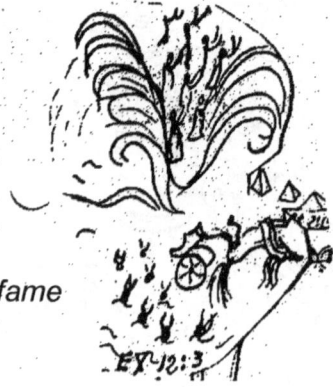

EX 42:3

Take off your shoes, you stand on holy ground
Our God came down to earth to set the Hebrews free,
For that commission a sheep herder was found
To guide His human sheep through the Red Sea.

Not me, my Elohim, I cannot speak
I falter and stutter so I cannot go,
I AM has called you and it's you I seek
With Aaron's help, free My people from their foe.

I'll show you miracles sublime to heed
So all of the people will see,
That I am powerful in awesome deed
You soon will learn to trust in Me.

Four hundred years their time was traced
With burdens heavy and mournful tone,
All ancient teachings once embraced
Through slavery godly knowledge gone.

The Hebrew people lost their rights
But God remembered them,
He sent old Moses to their plight
Oh, what will God do and when?

Deep in My heart I felt their cries
I'll show them that I AM still their God,
I've heard their groaning and their sighs
I'll keep My promise to them with Moses rod.

So Moses went to Pharaoh's court
Whose heart was hardened in dismay,
God through Moses many miracles performed
"I'll let the Hebrews go to their God and pray."

In haste a little lamb they slayed
And baked unleavened bread,
The lamb they learned to love three days
Its blood on the doorposts was spread.

But those remained alive who chose
To obey God's word that Moses gave,
The Angel of death had passed their home
Without the blood, the first-born found an early grave.

Away with you, you dreadful crowd
Oh, how Pharaoh hated them,
Away with you, pray to your God
The Egyptian ruler enraged recruited his men.

Behind, the whirling chariots ride
Up ahead the Sea of Reeds.
How will He save them from this sight?
Well, you know His awesome deeds!

The wind produced a pathway to flee
Divided water standing on each side,
The Hebrews passing through the sea
Our God showed His awesome might.

Today again, the Exodus but this time from the North
God's loving heart is yearning still,
Fishermen unite—God opens Israel's doors
Don't wait till hunters aim to kill—pack your bags—
                                    and do God's will.

His Glory Marks His Being

The universe, a secret held
    in God Almighty, planned;
The Holy Place, an equal space
    is fashioned by His hand.

The Star of David, an ensign formed
    His plan for us unfold,
Three sides, six times, forming a star
    a way to the One of old.

Right side to top: Almighty stands
    the Holy Spirit on His side,
Yeshua, Son, the lower bar
    He gave the world His light.

The inner star with concave curve
    Our fathers of three names
Abraham, Isaac and Jacob
    the start of Jewish fame.

Fathers, mothers, children
    are in the curve convected,
The inner point, an atom forms
    the universe compacted.

From the largest thing unsearchable
    to the smallest thing unseen,
There is no place without our God
    His glory marks His being.

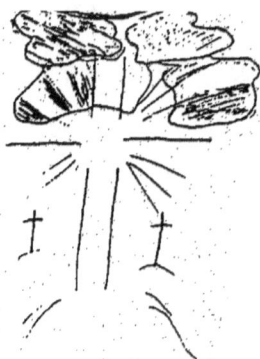

First Fruits

Long before the world was made
Our salvation plan was laid.

G – D so loved the world He gave His Son.
As Mary's babe His earthly life was begun.

Humbly in a Bethlehem stable born,
Unjust His death, His followers mourned.

Gloriously in three days He arose
Seen by His friends, the ones He chose.

His Resurrection was what Satan feared.
On the Feast of First Fruits He reappeared.

Yeshua, we kiss Your nail-scarred feet
You saved us from a world gone bad indeed.

Keep us sheltered by Your guiding hand
Till You take us to Your Promised Land.

Thank You, Yeshua, our G-D and friend
For life eternal with You we'll spend.

Yom Kippur

You chose that I would find You
After looking many years,
Uncounted ways were laid before me
I longed for You with flowing tears.

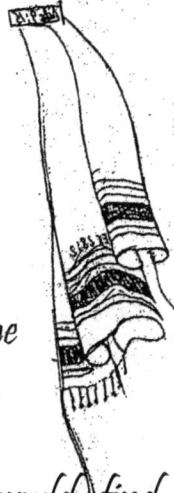

You promised by searching that I would find
The only One Who is the Truth,
That in my heart a void would be filled
By the anointed Jew of Jews.

Today on Yom Kippur I know
My crimson sins have all been purged,
And through His all-forgiving love
My life anew has now emerged.

With thankful heart, I praise my God
Who surrendered Himself, His life to give;
He suffered, died, and rose again
That you and I, in Him, may live.

The Wailing Wall

Stones that were hewn out in the quarry
Were quietly placed in the Temple walls
An ancient monument of former glory
Where He still hears our cries and calls

There is no other place to think of
Where once His glory filled the room;
But greater yet, He came to save us,
And gloriously walked from His tomb.

But yet today He still keeps loving
Jerusalem His scar-faced bride.
The tears He sees, the pleas He's hearing—
The Wailing Wall, oh humble sight.

They took the Temple and destroyed her—
No stone left in its place by Roman hands.
They plundered every nook and cranny—
The Western Wall a solemn monument.

There is no other place to mention
Where tears could lift the ocean tide,
Where hopes and dreams were left to ashes
Until the day He comes to take His bride.

"I will bless those who bless you" Gen 12:3

Our Home Group

God gave me a home to share
To which people come from everywhere,
We gather with hugs, have coffee or tea
We sing some songs, our love flows free.
We schmooze a bit and share our week
But sharing Yeshua is the peak,
We read the Bible and discuss
Finding out about God is our thrust.
We pray for friends and family
We care for each other—come and see,
If you want a touch of friendly folk
Come join our group and share a joke.
We gather weekly, our pattern is easy
Whether sun or rain or snow or breezy,
It shortens the week 'til the Sabbath day
Where we all come worship, sing and pray.
Feel free to call and join our group
And when I have time I make chicken soup.

Let's Be Women of Influence

Let us be women of influence, whatever God's call
We all leave a legacy, some famous, some small
We all have a destiny to leave behind
So in our pursuit, let's be helpful and kind.

One outstanding woman followed her call so severe
By offering herself, I am standing here.
She listened to Mordecai who urged her on
"It depends on you now, just be willing and strong.
I believe you were born for such a time as this
If you neglect God's plan you won't be missed."
But Esther, Hadassah, stood firm, braving the task.
Her unselfish deed saved the Jews at last.
With her courage she put on the gallows, Haman, that conniver.
And now I can praise God today as a holocaust survivor.

[To be a Jew is to be a praiser of God
But the word "Jew" most people understand it not.]

Golda Maier persevered with her shout
She depended on God and we, too, can't do without.
One day she stood before an influential group.
She said, "I will not beat around the bush. I'll give you the scoop.
A war is imminent to purge our land
To win it, on you it does depend."
Yes, the men followed her plea; Israel will always stand.

We, too, follow a heavenly throng
We can change our world in more ways than one.
We have to stand ready for whatever the call,
God knows what we are able—for a large task or small.

Every day counts; it is eleven forty-five.
It depends on us all for good to survive.

I don't want to scare you but please know where you stand
We live in a world that needs a hand.
Use your talents, your money, even yourself
Let your influence count before the clock strikes twelve.

Be ready on the day His task you are given
To work on our future for a more Godly living.
He'll show you the way and give you good sense.
So let's become women of great influence.

September 11

September 11 woke us up from a day as usual
Our world got changed—so unthinkable, so cruel,
A weapon made of our own passenger planes
Twin Towers fallen never to be seen again.

People falling, raining ashes and debris
A picture from hell I now must see.
Photos shown of missing loved ones, "Where have they gone?"
It's hard to believe that now they're in the dark beyond.

Our whole country saw the terror, stunned in unbelief
Three thousand murdered and America in grief,
So many families mourn, and a whole city torn
Death and destruction on that infamous Tuesday morn.

A nation under God—we ignored His call
September 11 woke us up from a day as usual,
America the beautiful, her faith is now in tears
A wake-up call to turn around after all these years.

We have seen destruction on so many a foreign shore
Now it has struck home, we're stunned in horror,
Satan reared his ugly head—he has no heart, no love, nor grace
But many heroes have emerged who tirelessly tried their faith.

Yet life must be lived and must go on
America the beautiful, her innocence gone;
Many faces, many hands—we will rebuild, we love this land
Oh gracious God, stand by us now, forgive, give us Your hand.

My G-D, Why?

"My G-D, why September 11's morn?"

"I'll tell you why, so many are killed before they were born.
You live a lifestyle not created for mankind.
I gave you the Bible but you closed your mind.
I withdrew the angels where I am not feared.
Once you were a "nation under G-D" but your belief has disap-
*   peared.*

"Come back to Me with repentant heart and you will see.
Turn from your wicked ways and come and pray to Me.
Pray for forgiveness, for your family and friends,
And I will hear your plea and heal your land."

"My G-D, will You restore us and awaken our faith again?"

"Faith comes from the Bible. You should read it all you can.
My child, I came to earth one day 2000 years ago.
I was rejected even then, but still I love you so.
The enemy stole your innocence and your walk with Me.
But if you turn around, My child, a better world you'll see."

"My G-D, my Lord, my Elohim, please take me by Your hand."

"O yes, My child, just trust in Me. I want to heal your land.
I'd like to do many things for you, to make a better place.
But where there is no trust in Me, I will withdraw My grace.
With fear and trembling you must now walk My way.
If you will see a peaceful land, repent, forgive and pray."

California is Burning
10-23-07

California is burning. Smoke fills the air
Houses offered to the flames of poor or millionaire.
Hordes try to conquer the fire's unquenchable appetite.
People now homeless. Who will stay at their side?

Why so many calamitous foes?
The fire burns. No water flows
Parched on one side, floods on the other.
Why G-D, please? Why these disasters?
Did You remove Your protection from America
Disaster I see from Mexico to Canada.
Is it because we turned our back on Israel?
So You call the storm and dry up our well?
"I bless who blesses you," You once said to Abram.
Have we twisted the prime minister's arm?
Have we let politics take precedent over Your will?
Now the U.S. is suffering and people get ill.
Have You taken Your blessings from us,
Now endure the consequences we must?

Awaiting the Storm

In midst of the ocean the monster was born

Roaring ferociously with increasing scorn,

It sucked up waters from deep below

Consuming all where it would go.

The news was ominous for the coastal state

It would wreak havoc on what comes in its wake,

The ocean swelled high driven on land

The wind's awesome fury threw bellows of sand.

So many lost lives—others their home

Afterward many through rubble will comb,

There is no weapon when nature is mad

Man has to reckon, the outcome is sad.

"There will be ... distress among nations confused by the roaring of the sea and the waves" (Luke 21:25).

Our Father

Our Father loves you endlessly
He knows you deep within,
There is no good or bad you've done
Of which He has not seen.

He laughs and smiles and cries with you
And always holds you up,
Cajoling you so tenderly
To lead you by His map.

This map, God's Holy Book
We read the story of mankind,
It tells us about His great love
And shows where we've been blind.

He gives us ways and days to keep
Gives gifts we cannot earn,
He urges diligence to read
His Holy Word to learn.

His love is flowing endlessly
He even gave His Son,
There'll come a day we'll see His face
And hear, "My child, well done."

My Savior

I love You, my Lord, my Savior

For love and forgiveness You stand,

I ask You to lead me through all my days

And stay with me 'til the end.

But the end of my life means beginning

With so much greater to come,

For then You'll give me joy of things

On earth I have never known.

'Til You Return

We daily pray against the foe
Only You know how it will go,
You have declared the things to come
You will be the triumphant One.

But 'til that time we must be strong
'Til all our enemies are gone,
The world will rage and we will yearn
'Til You, Yeshua, do return.

You are forever my great hope
Could I from this old world elope?
To be with You, my soul does long
'Til You return with Your heavenly throng.

www.ingramcontent.com/pod-product-compliance
Lightning Source LLC
LaVergne TN
LVHW061258060426
835508LV00015B/1413